THE ANT AND THE GRASSHOPPER

One day, an ant nearly got baked under the hot sun!

She was dragging grains of corn to store away for the winter.

A lazy grasshopper was watching the ant struggling so hard.

He said, "Winter is months away. Come and relax!"

"Oh! I cannot do that," replied the ant. "Time just flies!"

"You should also store some food for yourself," she suggested.

The grasshopper paid no attention to the ant. The ant went away.

The grasshopper idled through the summer. For him, there were no worries.

Soon it was winter. The weather became very cold.

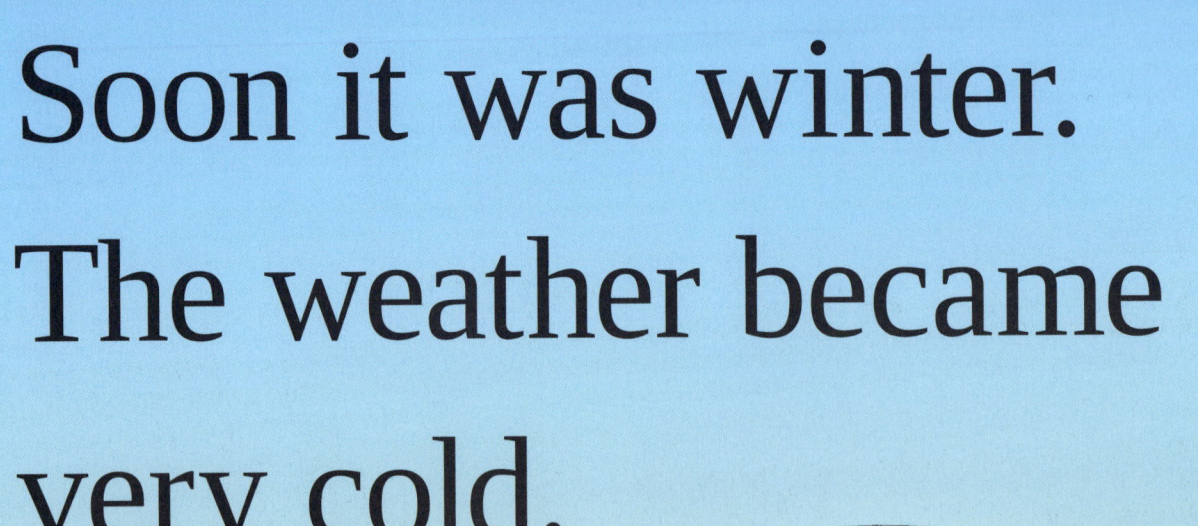

There was no food for the grasshopper!
His house was empty!

He went to the ant and begged her to give him some corn.

The ant refused, saying he should have stored it himself.

The foolish grasshopper went back hungry.
He felt sorry for himself.

He had not a crumb to eat, while the ant enjoyed plenty of food.

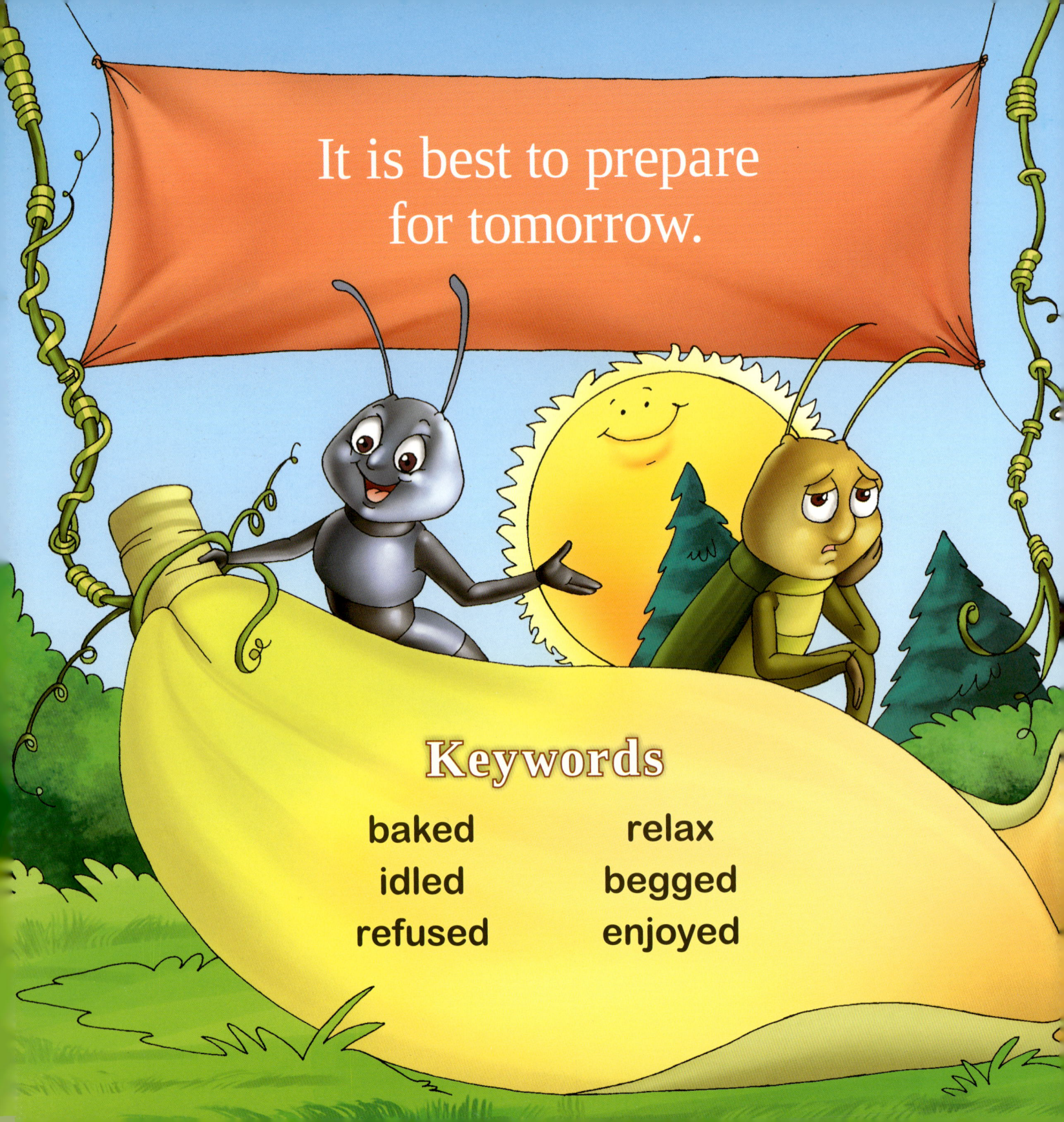